It's festival time . . .

The word for festival or party in Spanish is ***fiesta*** [*fee-AYS-tah*]. There is a *fiesta* somewhere in Mexico on every day of the year.

Most *fiestas* include music and dancing and good things to eat. Children celebrate with a ***piñata*** full of sweets. (You don't know what a *piñata* is? – find out on page 25.) Come along and join the party! It's festival time in Mexico . . .

Where's Mexico?

Mexico lies just south of the United States. Many years ago, the western part of the United States also belonged to Mexico, including California, Arizona, New Mexico, Colorado, Nevada, and Utah. The land of Mexico varies a lot. It ranges from snowy mountains and volcanoes to tropical rainforests and deserts. The capital, Mexico City, is one of the largest cities in the world.

This painting shows how Diego Rivera, a great Mexican artist, imagined the Aztec capital.

A Mexican girl holds a stack of that favourite Mexican food, tortillas.

Who are the Mexicans?

Most Mexicans are *mestizo* [*mess-TEE-zo*], a mixture of Spanish and native peoples. After Columbus came to America, explorers moved out into the new land. Hernán Cortés came to Mexico in 1519 and found the **Aztecs** living there. They had a beautiful city where Mexico City stands today. Traders came from all around to their markets.

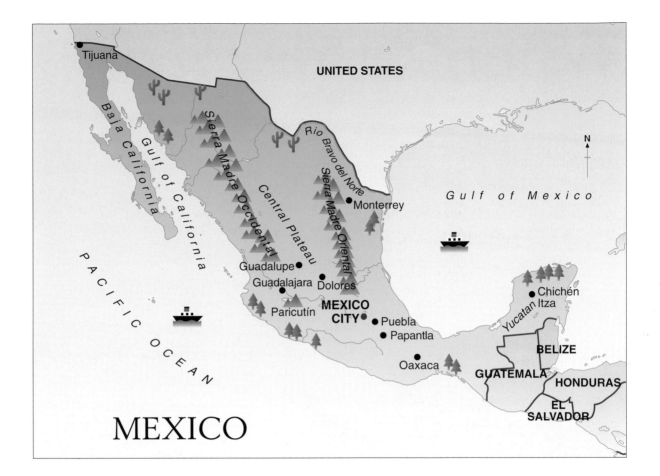

MEXICO

The Aztec leader, Montezuma, thought Cortés might be one of their gods returning. But he soon found that Cortés was only interested in getting their gold and silver. The Spanish conquered the Aztecs and made them work as slaves.

After a long time, the Spaniards and the native peoples mixed and created the *mestizo* people. Mexico today is also a mixture of Spanish and Aztec traditions.

The early people of Mexico built large pyramids like this one at Chichén Itza.

When's the *Fiesta?*

SPRING

- **Birthday of Benito Juáez**
- **Holy Week and Easter**
- **Labour Day**
- **Battle of Puebla** (*Cinco de Mayo*)

Are you scared yet? Come join me for Carnival on page 8.

SUMMER

- **Feast of Corpus Christi** – In Papantla, the *Voladores* [*vohl-ah-DOR-ays*] perform an ancient ritual where they drop off a high pole and swing in circles down to the ground.

- **St. John the Baptist's Day** People are baptized in a pool or fountain or by having water thrown on them.

- **Feast of Our Lady of Carmen** A flower festival with native dancing.

- **Feast of the Assumption** – On this day there is often a running of the bulls (look at the picture on page 17). Church doors are decorated with flowers.

6

Ride on over to page 19 for Independence Day.

Go ahead – make my day (the Day of the Dead, that is). Join me on page 22.

AUTUMN

- **Independence Day**
- *Día de la Raza* (Day of the Race) – The day when Columbus landed in the New World. Mexicans celebrate this day as the beginning of the *mestizo* people from the mixing of Spanish and native peoples.
- **Day of the Dead**
- **Revolution Day** – There is a big parade of athletes in Mexico City to celebrate the Mexican Revolution of 1910.

WINTER

- **Feast of the Virgin of Guadalupe**
- *Navidad* (Christmas)
- **New Year's Day**
- **Epiphany (Three Kings' Day)**
- **St. Anthony's Day** – Children put ribbons and flowers on their pets and take them to the church to be blessed.
- *Día de la Candelaria* – Candles, and seeds for planting, are blessed in the churches.
- **Carnival**

Feliz Navidad! We're having a Christmas party on pages 24 and 25.

Carnival and Easter

Mexican festivals are full of colour and excitement. Probably the most exciting and colourful is Carnival. Carnival is celebrated in many Catholic countries. Catholics used to fast during the day for 40 days before Easter.

This was called Lent.

Before starting this long fast, people celebrated with a big festival. Today Catholics don't generally fast for the entire time of Lent, but they still celebrate Carnival in many countries.

A day of surprises

Carnival is a time when anything can happen. As you walk down the street, you bump into people wearing masks and fantastic costumes. Fireworks explode all around. Musicians play tunes as they stroll along. There are always parades. Brightly decorated floats move down the main street carrying people in costumes.

These children are dressed up as Mexican soldiers for Carnival.

8

Different kinds of battles

Women and children sometimes have flower battles for Carnival. They line up and throw flowers at each other and at anyone else standing around.

Children also like to have egg battles. They blow out the eggs and fill the shells with confetti. Then the children form two lines. They walk past each other and try to break their eggs on each other's heads as they pass.

These people are dressed up as Spanish conquerors, called **conquistadores** [*kon-kee-sta-DOR-ays*]. A long time ago, the native peoples used Carnival as a chance to make fun of the Spanish. These costumes are now part of the tradition of Carnival.

Easter

Easter comes after the fasting time of Lent. It is an important holiday in Mexico. At this time Mexicans think about Jesus's sacrifice. There are special ceremonies at the church. Mexicans also celebrate with singing and dancing, and there are a lot of special foods to eat.

Above: On Good Friday, the day when Jesus was crucified, Mexicans put on a play of his death. The drama takes place in the town square.

Right: These people are taking part in the Good Friday procession. They wear hoods to show they are sorry for their sins.

Setting Judas on fire

A special Mexican Easter tradition is to hang a **papier-mâché** model of Judas, the person who betrayed Jesus, from a balcony. Often he is made to look like someone people don't like.

Strings of firecrackers are wound around the Judas and candles and toys are tied to it.

On Saturday morning at 10.00 am, the church bells start to ring, and the firecrackers are lit. As the firecrackers explode, they set the Judas figure on fire. The toys and sweets fall, and children rush to grab the treats.

Lighting the fireworks on a Judas figure for Easter in a small town in Mexico.

Think about this

Mexicans like to dress up as Spanish **conquistadores** for Carnival. Do you ever dress up like a famous person to poke fun at them? Have you seen other people do this for a festival? Do you ever dress up like people from history?

The Feast of Our Lady of Guadalupe

Guadalupe is a little town in central Mexico. Find it on the map on page 5. If you found yourself there on 12 December, you would see crowds of people going to the main square in front of the church. Let's follow them. There's music coming from the square. You can smell the *tacos, tostadas*, and *tamales* from the food stalls around the square. Now you can see the dancers with their feather head-dresses. These are **conchero** [*cone-CHAY-roh*] dancers. *Conchero* comes from the word *concha*, which means shell in Spanish. These dancers wear bracelets of shells around their ankles. The shells make a rhythm as they dance.

Left: Boys dress up like **peasants** for the festival. They wear a **serape** [*say-RAH-pay*], which is a colourful blanket worn by peasants, and sandals and a false moustache. Or they might wear white trousers and a white shirt with a mask. They are called *Dieguitos* [*dee-ay-GEE-tohs*], which means Little Diegos. Who's Diego? Read the story on page 15.

Right: These *conchero* dancers are making a rhythm with their sticks.

A long walk

On the day of the *fiesta*, millions of people make a **pilgrimage** to Guadalupe to thank Our Lady of Guadalupe for answering their prayers. They come from all around. Some walk for days or ride their bicycles from far away to get there. Who is Our Lady of Guadalupe?

Left: **Conchero** dancers for the Feast of Our Lady of Guadalupe imitate the way the **Aztecs** used to dress for festivals. They wear feather head-dresses, and bells and shells around their ankles.

Above right: Climbing the steps to the Shrine of Our Lady of Guadalupe.

Listen to a story . . .

One morning in 1531 (that's 40 years after Columbus came to America), a **peasant** named Juan Diego was on his way to church when a lovely lady looking like a native Mexican appeared before him. She said that she was the Virgin Mary, and she asked Juan to tell the local bishop to build a church in her honour. When Juan told the bishop about this, he said Juan was crazy. The next day the Virgin appeared again. She told Juan to pick some roses from a special spot where they had never grown before. Juan went and found roses growing there. He wrapped them in his *serape* and brought them to the bishop. When he opened the *serape*, there was a picture of the Virgin printed on the inside. The bishop then built the shrine and put the *serape* in it. You can still see the *serape* there today.

People quietly pray to the Virgin at the shrine in her honour.

Think about this

The Festival of Our Lady of Guadalupe is on the same day as an older festival for an Aztec goddess. Often Christian festivals take the place of earlier festivals. When people became Christian, they changed their old festivals to new ones, but they kept many of the old customs. Do you know who gave out presents before Santa Claus? (Give up? Look on page 26.)

A very Mexican saint

Mexicans are very fond of the Virgin of Guadalupe. Many people come every year to ask her for favours or thank her for helping them. You can see her picture all over when you go to Mexico, just like the one on this page. Mexicans feel that the Virgin showed she cared about them by making herself look like a native Mexican. They feel she is one of them.

Celebrating Mexico

There are some holidays when Mexicans remember people who made a difference to their country. On 21 March, Mexicans celebrate the birthday of their best-loved leader, Benito Juárez. Juárez was a Zapotec (that's one of the many groups of native Mexicans). His parents died when he was three years old. He was poor when he was young, but he worked hard to get ahead. In 1861 he became the first native president of Mexico. Juárez always worked to help the poor people of Mexico, especially the native peoples. He freed them from working on the haciendas, large farms where they worked almost as slaves.

A portrait of Benito Juárez.

Left: Another holiday celebrates Benito Juárez: the *Cinco de Mayo*. *Cinco de Mayo* means 5th May in Spanish, and that is the day when Benito Juárez and his army beat the French at the Battle of Puebla, when the French were trying to take over Mexico.

Right: A running of the bulls. A bull is let loose in the main street of the town, and brave people get a chance to try their skill in bullfighting.

Do Mexicans have an Independence Day?

Mexico celebrates its independence on 16 September every year. That isn't really the day Mexico became independent. It's the day when it all started.

A painting of Father Hidalgo by Diego Rivera. On Independence Day, people remember Father Hidalgo, who started the independence movement.

A long time ago . . .

Father Miguel Hidalgo y Costilla was a priest in the little town of Dolores. He and many other Mexicans felt unfairly treated by Spain, and that Mexico should be independent. So they planned a revolution. On 16 September, Father Hidalgo started ringing the church bells. When the people came, he told them about his plans. At the end he shouted, *'Viva México! Viva la independencia!'* That means 'Long live Mexico! Long live independence!' The people took any weapons they could find and marched with him. More and more people joined them along the way. This was the start of the Mexican Revolution.

An Independence Day parade.

What happens on Independence Day?

On 16 September every year, Mexico's president steps out on the balcony of the National Palace and cries, *'Viva México! Viva la independencia!'* The crowd replies, *'Viva México! Viva la independencia!'* The mayors of all the towns in Mexico do the same. Then everyone throws confetti, and the celebrations begin.

Charros are skillful riders who perform daring feats with a horse and lasso. Going to see *charros* perform is a favourite way to celebrate Independence Day.

The Day of The Dead

A group of people in long robes are marching down the main street. They are carrying a coffin. Suddenly the coffin opens and a skeleton pops out.

It is 1 November in Mexico, and this is a procession for the Day of the Dead. People everywhere dress as ghosts, skeletons or witches. The markets are all full of toy skeletons and sweets that look like little skulls. Children eat skulls with their name on the forehead.

Above: Chocolate skulls on sale at a market.

Right: A woman puts the finishing touches on an altar decorated with flowers and candles.

What is the Day of the Dead?

For Christians around the world, 1 November is All Saints' Day. The Mexicans call this day the Day of the Dead. Mexicans believe that the spirits of people who have died return to the world of the living at this time.

Waiting for the dead

People prepare by going to the graves of their relatives. They sweep and clean the grave and lay flowers on it. They put out the dead person's favourite foods and drinks, and candles and incense to lead the spirit back. Then they keep watch by the grave all night, waiting for the spirits to return. The souls of children who have died return on the night of 31 October. They are called the *muertitos chicos* [*mwer-TEE-toes CHEE-kohs*], the 'dear little dead ones'. People leave out toys, cakes, and hot chocolate to sweeten their return. The next night the adults return. After feeding the dead, everyone returns to the house and eats a big meal to celebrate life.

Music for the ghosts

Sometimes people even provide music for the returning spirits, so you might find a *mariachi* band playing in the corner of the graveyard. *Mariachi* bands started about 100 years ago. *Mariachi* is typically Mexican music.

This skeleton is dressed up in the costume of a soldier in the Mexican revolution. Look at his **sombrero**, the big hat with flowers embroidered on it.

People talk while waiting for the dead to return. They've decorated the graves with marigolds and candles. The **Aztecs** believed marigolds were the flowers of the dead.

Mariachis wear tight black trousers and short black jackets with silver studs on the sides. They may also wear large *sombreros*.

Think about this

The eve of the Day of the Dead is celebrated in Britain as Halloween. Do you see any differences between Halloween and the Day of the Dead or any things that are the same?

Navidad

*N*avidad [*nah-vee-DAD*] is Spanish for Christmas. Mexicans wish each other *'Feliz Navidad'* [*fay-LEES nah-vee-DAD*] around Christmas time. Mexican children do many of the same things for Christmas that children do in Britain. They decorate Christmas trees, and they visit Santa Claus. Traditionally, they get their presents on 6 January, the day when the three wise men brought gifts to the infant Jesus. They leave their shoes by the door along with water for the wise men's camels. In the morning, the water is gone and the shoes are full of presents. Today they often get gifts at Christmas, too.

Children getting their picture taken with Santa Claus. Have you ever done this?

Looking for shelter

Mexicans also have some Christmas traditions that we don't, like *posada* [*poh-SAH-dah*] processions. *Posada* means rest, and this tradition relives Mary and Joseph's search for a place to rest. Groups of children go from door to door around their neighbourhood. Two of the children are dressed up like Mary and Joseph. At each house, they sing, 'I am tired. I beg for rest.' From inside the house other children sing, 'Go away, go away, there is no room.' They keep on until they get to a house where they are let in. There they have a Christmas party.

Children in a *posada* procession with a real donkey.

How to have a *piñata* party

Trying to break the *piñata* at a party. *Piñatas* are popular at Christmas parties, birthdays and all kinds of **fiestas**.

Piñatas [*pee-NYAH-tas*] are made of either clay or **papier-mâché** covered with curls of tissue. They are filled with sweets and, sometimes, small toys. *Piñatas* come in many different shapes, from traditional Christmas stars to Batman figures.

At a party, the *piñata* is hung from a tree just out of reach. An adult holds the rope to move the *piñata* up and down. A child is blindfolded. He or she takes a bat and tries to hit the *piñata*. Each child takes a turn until someone breaks the *piñata*, and the sweets spill out on the ground.

Then everyone runs to grab as many sweets as they can.

Things you can do

If you were in Mexico on Independence Day, you might celebrate by having a cup of Mexican Hot Chocolate with *galletas* [*gah-YAY-tahs*] – those are Mexican biscuits. Look for some in a Mexican market, or try making your own by decorating plain biscuits with red, white and green icing or sweets.

Sing a cockroach song

You could also try singing *'La Cucaracha'* [*lah koo-kah-RAH-cha*]. You may know the song already, but did you know that it's about a cockroach? And did you know that it's also about Pancho Villa, who was a hero of the Mexican Revolution? The song says that the prettiest girl to travel with Pancho Villa was a cockroach with no legs. Here are the words in Spanish and English, with guides to help you sing it in Spanish.

Make Mexican Hot Chocolate

Mix these in a cup:
1 teaspoon cocoa
3 teaspoons sugar
⅓ cup powdered milk
½ teaspoon cinnamon
Fill the cup with hot water and stir. Put 1 tablespoon of whipped cream on top.
Or, when you're in a Mexican market, look for bars of Mexican chocolate and a *molinillo* [moh-lee-NEE-yo]—that's a wooden beater that you twirl between your palms to break up the chocolate.

Answer to page 15
Before Christian times, the pagan god Odin visited earth around the end of December to reward good and punish evil. Saint Nicholas, later Santa Claus, took over his duties.

La Cucaracha

The lit - tle cock - roach, the lit - tle cock - roach,
La cu - ca - ra - cha, la cu - ca - ra - cha,
la koo - ka - ra - cha, la koo - ka - ra - cha

Can - not walk u - pon her
Ya no pue - de ca - mi
ya no pway - day ka - mee -

legs, Be - cause she lost them, be - cause she lost them,
nar, Por - que no tie - ne, por - que le fal - tan,
nar por - kay no tyen - nay por - kay lay fal - tan

All her lit - tle jet black
Las pa - ti - tas de a -
las pa - tee - tas del a -

legs. Gentlemen this lit - tle bee - tle,
trás. La cu - ca - ra - cha se - ño - res,
trass la koo - ka - ra - cha sain - yor - ays

She was eve - ry - bo - dy's dar - ling,
Siem - pre fue u - na mas co - ti - lla,
syem - pray fwayoo - na mas - ko - tee - ya

And she was the pret - ty girl who
Y'a de - más lin - da mu - cha - cha
eeya day - mass lin - da moo - cha - cha

Pancho Vil - la brought a - round.
Que lle - va - ba Pan - cho Villa.
kay lyay - ba - ba pan - cho beeya

Things to look for in your library

World of Festivals: Christmas Catherine Chambers, Evans 1996
The World of Festivals Philip Steele, Macdonald Young Books 1996
Season Festivals: Autumn/Winter/Spring/Summer Wayland 1990
Country Fact Files: Mexico Macdonald Young Books 1996
World Focus: Mexico Rob Alcraft & Sean Sprague, Heinemann Library 1996
Mexico Anna Lewington, Wayland 1996
Celebrate: Christian Festivals Jan Thompson, Heinemann Publishers 1995
Discovering Religions: Christianity Sue Penny, Heinemann Library 1995
Discovering Sacred Texts: The Christian Bible W. Owen Cole, Heinemann Library 1995
World Religions: Christianity John Logan, Wayland 1995
High Days and Holidays: Celebrating the Christian Year David Self, Lion Publishers 1993
Heinemann Stories from World Religions Heinemann Educational 1995

Make an Aztec shield

Make your own **Aztec** shield like the one the *conchero* dancers carry in the Festival of Our Lady of Guadalupe. You can choose a Mexican picture or make your own drawing.

This shield is made using wool, in the style of wool paintings made by the Huichol people, who live on the Pacific Coast of Mexico. If you don't want to use wool, you can just paint your picture on the shield.

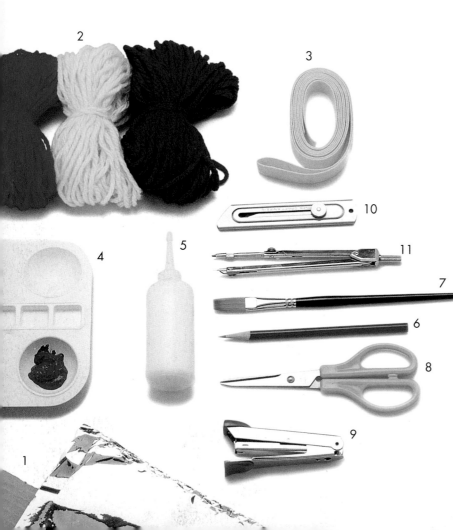

You will need

1 Cardboard and gold foil paper
2 Balls of heavy wool
3 Elastic
4 Tempera paint
5 Glue
6 Pencil
7 Brushes
8 Scissors
9 Stapler
10 Craft knife
11 Compass

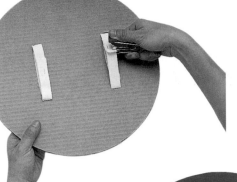

2 Cut the cardboard in a circle. Cut slits in the shield and put elastic through them. Cut the elastic and staple it in the back so that it fits over your arm.

1 Draw the outline of a plant, animal, person or other shape in the centre of the cardboard square.

3 Paint around your drawing with the colour you want your shield to be.

4 Put glue on the outline and press wool into the glue, one or two strands at a time. Spread glue inside the shape and press wool into it. Use one or two strands of wool at a time and follow the shape of the outline. Use different colours.

5 Cut a circle from the foil to fit around the edge of the shield and glue it in place. Cut it to make a fringe. Make a border by spreading glue around the edges of the shield. Press wool along the edges, making different coloured stripes.

Make *guacamole*

Favourite foods at festivals are *tamales*, *tostadas* and *tacos*. These are all made with *tortillas*, which are like thin corn pancakes. Mexicans eat *tortillas* with almost every meal. Mexican food is mostly made of different variations of corn, beans and rice. These three together along with some fruits and vegetables make a healthy diet.

Another favourite festival food is *guacamole* [*gwah-kah-MOE-lay*]. You can make *guacamole* easily at home. Here's how.

You will need

1. 2 ripe avocados
2. Half a small onion
3. 2–3 sprigs fresh coriander
4. 1 chilli pepper (if you like it spicy)
5. 2 tomatoes
6. 2 tablespoons lemon juice
7. Salt
8. Spoon
9. Fork
10. Bowl
11. Knife
12. Measuring spoons

1 Cut the avocados in half, take out the stones, and scoop out the avocado.

2 Put the avocado in a bowl and mash it up with a fork.

3 Chop up the onion, coriander, pepper and tomatoes. Add them all to the avocado.

4 Add the lemon juice and a little salt until it tastes right. Mix it well. Dip in your tortilla chips and eat!

Glossary

Aztecs	*people who lived in Mexico when the Spanish came*
charro	*a person who performs tricks on horseback for a rodeo*
conchero	*a dancer who wears shells around his ankles*
conquistador	*a person who wins a war against someone else*
fiesta	*a festival or party*
mariachi	*a type of music from Mexico*
mestizo	*people who are part Spanish and part native*
papier-mâché	*made of layers of paper dipped in flour water and dried*
peasant	*a poor farmer*
pilgrimage	*a trip to a holy place*
piñata	*a papier-mâché or clay figure filled with sweets*
serape	*a colourful blanket worn by peasants*
sombrero	*a hat*

Index